RISKY BUSINESS

TRUSTED BY HOSPITALITY LEADERS

"David has a unique understanding of the restaurant industry enabling him to offer his restaurant clients a quality insurance product at a competitive price. Ambassador Group Insurance is synonymous with trust, character and dependability… the values David demonstrates to his clients on a daily basis. He is a true industry friend and the Arizona Restaurant Association gladly endorses him as a provider for Property and Casualty Insurance."

Steve Chucri
President & CEO
Arizona Restaurant Association

"David DeLorenzo was the first insurance broker I worked with in Arizona and twelve years later I have never thought of making a change. His business philosophy is understanding your business and doing what is in your best interest. Whether a single unit operation or multiple-units nationwide, David and his team have solutions for your insurance needs. When other business owners ask me for a recommendation on a vendor, the first name I give them is David DeLorenzo and The Ambassador Group."

Andrew F. Diamond
President
Angry Crab Franchise, LLC

"An outstanding partner for my businesses, providing exceptional service and support. Their friendly and knowledgeable approach has been particularly beneficial for my brewery, restaurant, and coffee shop operations. They understand the unique challenges and requirements of our industry, and their tailored solutions have been invaluable. The entire team is always available to address my questions and concerns, ensuring we have the right coverage to protect my businesses."

Nick Campisano
Clever Koi - Born & Raised Hospitality

"Dave and his team have been great partners. They are always updating me on the newest products and helping me understand the coverages needed in our ever-changing industry. They are a great partner whether you are one restaurant or a growing company."

Jon Lane
O.H.S.O Brewery & Distillery

"Dave does a great job for our company and we trust him with our insurance needs. We feel confident in the work he does as well as his very competitive pricing. It is so nice to know that we can count on Dave and his staff to take care of our insurance so that we can spend more time taking care of our customers."

Tim Vasquez
President
Someburros! and Isabel's Amor

"Dave is very dedicated to the restaurant industry and has a lot of passion for doing the right thing at all times. He helps find coverage in reputable companies that help protect my establishments while getting me the best rates."

Barrett Rinzler
Cold Beers & Cheeseburgers

Thanks David! Partnering with you and your team for our insurance coverage was one of the best decisions ever! Looking forward to continuing a fruitful relationship for years to come!

Brian Jones
CEO
Carolinas Mexican Restaurants

"I can attest to the fact that Dave is very knowledgeable about insuring restaurants and bars. He has handled the insurance for six businesses for me up to this point in addition to my personal insurance needs and I will definitely continue to use him."

Julian Wright
Pedal Haus

"DeLo and The Ambassador Group have been an important part of our success at Barter & Shake. Managing risk in an effective but cost-conscious way is essential for any business, particularly for the bar business. He is a true leader in the space and his team is thoughtful in tailoring our coverage and proactive about finding the best combination of coverage and pricing."

Jeff Holland
Barter & Shake

RISKY BUSINESS

THE ARIZONA LIQUOR LIABILITY AND INSURANCE SURVIVAL GUIDE FOR BAR AND RESTAURANT OWNERS

BY DAVID DELORENZO
A.K.A. THE DELO

ISBN 979-8-234-04550-8

Portions of this book were developed with the assistance of artificial intelligence tools used for research support, drafting assistance, and editorial refinement. All content has been reviewed and approved by the author, and all opinions and conclusions expressed are solely those of the author.

I never thought that growing up a child of the 80's and getting a job for my favorite artists in the music business, I would turn to being an insurance broker. It was not a stretch because my father has been in the industry now 50 years. It just was not on my highly desired career list. After 25 years of doing insurance and finding my way into the hospitality niche. I know I found my calling. The ability to laser focus on an industry. The Hospitality Industry. How do I know when it's love? When I can't get enough, learning, educating, and growing. This book is just a small example of some of the in's and out's of the industry I have seen over the years. The men and women I have teamed up with over the years is who I owe the real thank you to. The attorneys, insurance companies, adjusters, trainers, lobbyist, hospitality establishments, and of course my coworkers and family. None of this happens without all of us. Cheers to the journey and may it continue for another 25 years.

CONTENTS

INTRODUCTION

THE REAL AND RAW SIDE OF HOSPITALITY: LIABILITY, LAW, AND LUCK

If you own a bar or restaurant, you already know this industry is not for the faint of heart. It's fast-paced, unpredictable, and full of long nights and tight margins. But while you're focused on menus, staffing, and keeping the doors open, there's a side of the business that doesn't always get the spotlight: what happens when something goes wrong.

This book will pull back the curtain on real-life insurance claims from bars and restaurants. Fires, fights, slip-and-falls, employee mishaps, and even the occasional freak accident are the headlines of stories that don't show up on your Instagram feed, but they are the ones that put your business at risk in the blink of an eye.

The goal of these stories isn't to scare you. They are to show you what can happen, what does happen, and what you can do to protect yourself, your business, and your staff. Each chapter shares a real story. They are short, informative, and maybe a little tragic or outrageous. But every story offers a lesson to ensure these things never happen in your establishment or on your watch.

Because in the bar and restaurant world, the best kind of insurance isn't just a policy, it's peace of mind. So, let's dive into the stories behind claims. But first, let me introduce myself...

WHO IS THE DELO?

Hey, that's me! I'm David DeLorenzo, but most people know me as the DELO. I started my career in the music industry and eventually started my own business, Diamond in the Rough Marketing. I loved promoting artists and the lifestyle that came with it. But the music business began to transition. People were buying albums online and downloading them to their computers. The company started losing momentum and was no longer sustainable.

I've always been close with my dad, so I decided to join him in the insurance industry at his company, Ambassador Group Insurance. I started out as an agent, with no money and no salary... and in all honesty, not a lot of passion for the job.

But one day everything changed when I was at a friend's restaurant, and he gave me his policy to review. The hospitality industry has a very similar culture to the music industry. It spoke to me. I wrote that policy for my friend, and he encouraged me to create a niche within my dad's business. Bar and Restaurant Insurance was born, and it sparked a passion for my career, and for helping the people in this industry.

I learned so much over the next three years and engulfed myself in this industry. I did everything I could to become more successful in this industry so I could get my name out there, build my brand, and create the tools, resources, and connections that I saw were so needed in the industry.

I wanted more than to be a friend or a vendor. I wanted a real relationship with my clients. So the more successful I became, the more money I invested in local restaurants. I did everything from passively investing to serving drinks. In total, I invested in 13 restaurants over the years.

This literally bought me an education in the industry from every angle. I was running the agency, writing insurance risk policies, and learning day by day the intricacies of what insurance companies were, and more importantly were not willing to cover when it came to exposures. With this experience, I could understand both sides of the coin, from the perspective of bar and restaurant owners and from the perspective of the insurance companies.

All that brought me to where I am today, with more than 600 restaurants under our agency's umbrella and a multitude of those who have been with me for two decades. We've watched each other grow. And helping them create programs and coverages has allowed me to become a true partner whom they trust. They know that my team and I will take care of them and protect them.

That is why I wrote this book. I want to help, protect, and connect as many people as I can, especially as the industry continues to change. In particular, the liquor liability aspect of bar and restaurant ownership has changed dramatically. Bar and restaurant owners need to protect themselves. They need to educate themselves. I hope this book serves as a valuable resource for bar and restaurant owners.

I AM THE DeJo

Your connector and protector.
I can't wait to serve you.

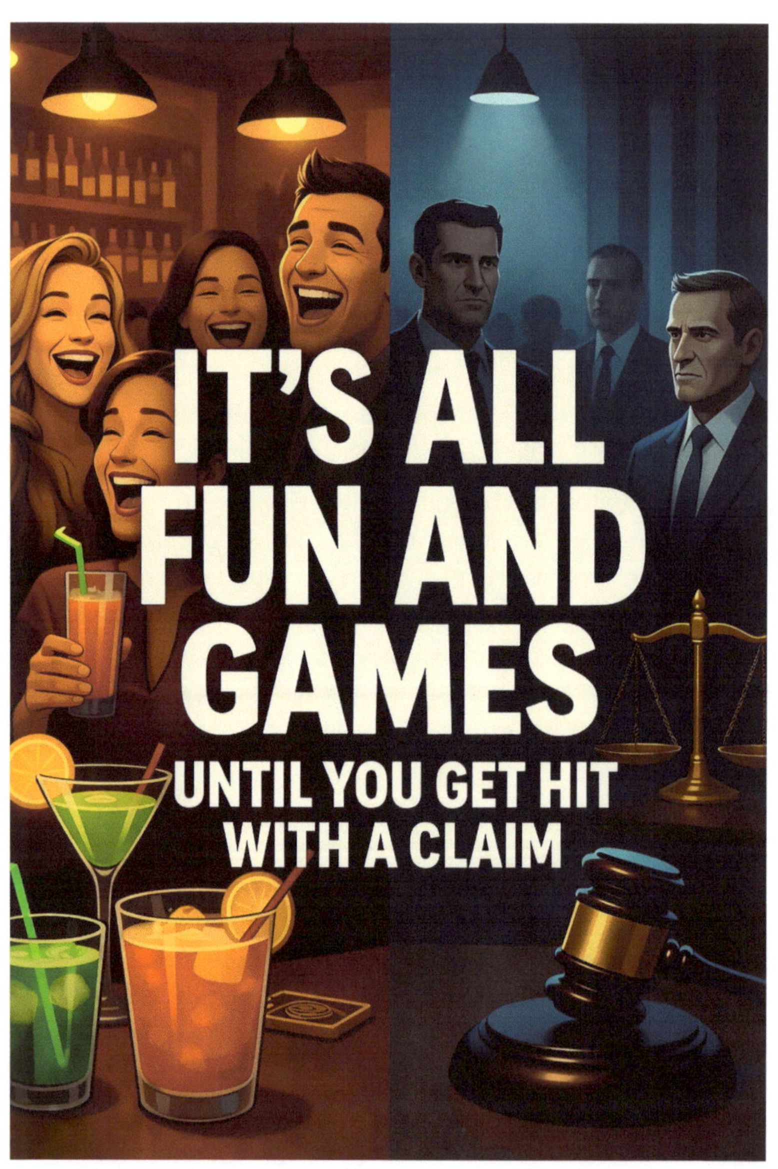
IT'S ALL
FUN AND
GAMES
UNTIL YOU GET HIT
WITH A CLAIM

SECTION ONE: REAL STORIES FROM THE BAR AND RESTAURANT INDUSTRY

FROM FUN AND GAMES TO STICKY CLAIMS

Whether you are a veteran in the business or are getting ready to open your first establishment, I hope you find insight, value, and gratitude within these pages.

And if you still have questions by the end of this book, reach out to me! In this chapter, we'll reveal some of the craziest stories local lawyers and bar and restaurant owners have witnessed. Some of it is brutal, some of it is unbelievable. But within each experience is a real lesson about the gravity of operating a business that sells alcohol and how crucial it is for restaurateurs to abide by the laws to protect themselves, their staff, and their patrons.

A customer, already showing signs of intoxication, came into a dive bar. Despite that, the bar served him a couple of drinks. Without warning, things took a turn that no one could have predicted. The man walked to the back of the bar and forcefully attempted to kiss a woman without her consent. She was seated beside her boyfriend, who immediately reacted, shoving the man out the door with a single punch.

"Without warning, things took a turn no one could have predicted."

Outside, the intoxicated man fell and struck his head on a concrete parking block, suffering a serious and potentially permanent cervical spine injury.

What could save the case: The entire incident was caught on video. Every moment, from the unwanted advance to the boyfriend's reaction and the tragic fall, was recorded by the bar's security cameras.

The core question is: What responsibility does the bar hold for what happened? The event unfolded in mere seconds. There was no physical altercation between the customer and staff, but is the bar to blame for failing to protect patrons from foreseeable harm?

In this case, the legal strategy hinges on the clear footage. It documents the man's behavior in real-time, including the unwanted physical contact, which the legal team is framing as sexual assault. They believe that most juries would agree that the man's actions triggered the chain of events that followed.

While tragic, this case is a sobering reminder that bars and restaurants must be vigilant. They need to focus not just on over-serving, but also on having the systems and training in place to respond when things escalate fast.

Lessons from the law:
This situation emphasizes the importance of video. This may become a sexual assault case, and regardless of how quickly the series of events escalated, it began with this man's actions: an unwanted and aggressive advance on this woman.

DELO'S TAKE: Based on the simple facts of this story, we're going to assume the aggressor was likely intoxicated. This could have been prevented by having security at the door, preventing anyone already under the influence from entering the bar. This also could have been prevented if servers had kept a close eye on how much these individuals were drinking. Further security outside or within the bar itself to mitigate any aggression.

TIPS TO PREVENT THIS KIND OF THING FROM HAPPENING:

- Monitor intoxicated patrons closely, and don't hesitate to cut them off or remove them if necessary.
- Train staff on signs of intoxication in patrons and intervention strategies for inappropriate behavior or potential altercations.
- Install and maintain security cameras with long-term footage storage (at least 30 days or up to a year). In this case, the video will prove to be a critical piece of evidence.
- Document everything from drink logs to incident reports. These small actions can make a big difference when a claim is filed.

WHERE EVERYBODY KNOWS YOUR NAME

THE POWER OF FAMILIAR FACES

Cue the old "Cheers" theme song... For many neighborhood bars, that isn't just a catchy tune reminiscent of the long-running show. It's a reality, and it's what keeps many customers coming back for more. Regulars walk in, bartenders greet them by name, pour their favorite drink, and maybe even throw in a joke. But there's more behind this simple exchange than good vibes and return visits. In the hospitality industry, especially in bars and neighborhood restaurants, knowing your customers can help protect your business from severe legal and financial fallout.

Take one local dive bar that has deep community roots. Over the years, they've dealt with a few claims. Still, interestingly, most of these cases were easily manageable, not because the incidents didn't happen, but because the staff knew their clientele. In fact, they knew them so well that they could give detailed, credible, and persuasive testimony. "I've been serving 'Big Mike' for ten years. I know what he's like when he's drunk. He wasn't drunk that night." That's powerful testimony for a jury.

> ***"I know what he's like when he's drunk. He wasn't drunk that night."***

Now compare that to high-volume spots in tourist zones, like the bars in Old Town Scottsdale or around the downtown sports stadiums, where patrons are often strangers.

When something goes wrong there, it's harder to gauge what "normal" behavior looks like for a customer. And it's nearly impossible to say whether someone was showing signs of intoxication because the staff has never seen them before.

Lessons from the law: While a bar or restaurant with a hefty crew of regulars can benefit from recognizing when those patrons' behavior begins to stray from the norm, establishments that see a more transient or tourist crowd may not always have that same benefit. That's where proper training on not only recognizing the signs of intoxication or over-consumption, but also how to effectively curb a patron's drinking and prevent a possible situation before it occurs.

DELO'S TAKE: Create a "Cheers"-like environment in your bar or restaurant with the following tips:

- Encourage staff consistency. The longer your staff sticks around, the more familiar they'll become with your regulars, and vice versa.
- Offer discounts or loyalty programs. Discounts, special offers, or "locals only deals" may encourage customers to go from popping in every now and then to becoming regulars.
- Train staff to engage with customers.
- When your staff builds rapport with customers, like a server remembering a favorite drink or usual order, regulars feel special, and that feeling is often what keeps them coming back.
- Build the kind of place where everyone knows each other's name. Not just for nostalgia, but because it's the smart thing to do.

GIRL, "DON'T GO AWAY MAD"

(JUST GO AWAY)

WHY VIDEO MATTERS

In the chaos of a busy night at a bar, situations can escalate fast, and if your staff isn't properly trained, a minor incident can turn into a major lawsuit.

Take this real-world scenario: A woman exits a Tempe bar, drink in hand. Security tells her she can't leave the premises with alcohol and must return inside or dispose of it. Her version of the story? She says she didn't throw her drink away and was then assaulted by the bouncer, resulting in a fractured hip and other injuries.

But the video told a very different story. The footage clearly showed the woman initiating the physical confrontation, swinging first, and attacking security before being restrained. Throughout the case, she maintained she didn't start it, but the video told the truth.

After taking several punches, the male bouncer defended himself with one hit. She went down hard. The plaintiff's attorney argued excessive force and inadequate staff training. And while there was ultimately a payout, the damages were far less than they would have been without video evidence, because the footage proved she was the aggressor.

Without that video, this would have been a classic "he said, she said" case between a male bouncer and a female patron. It could have been a much bigger uphill battle with a potentially massive settlement.

Lessons from the law:
In the absence of proper training and video evidence, even a justified response by your staff can look like misconduct. Invest in both, because in today's legal climate, they're your only defense.

instinctively, it can cost your business and potentially put staff and patrons in danger.

DELO'S TAKE:

There are several key factors to dissect in this situation:

- **Train for de-escalation:** Teach staff to avoid physical confrontation whenever possible. If someone becomes aggressive, hands off should be the rule. Calling the authorities is often the safest move.
- **Surveillance is non-negotiable:** "You're never winning if there's no video." Had this bar not had video, the case outcome would have been very different. Always maintain timestamped footage for at least 30 days, and longer if possible.
- **Know the biases:** Juries often sympathize with female patrons over male security, especially when alcohol is involved. The odds tilt heavily against you unless you have concrete evidence.
- **Clear protocols protect everyone:** Employees must know what to do when guests become non-compliant. If they panic or react

YOU GOT THE LOOK

LOOK FOR SIGNS OF OBVIOUS INTOXICATION

From a legal standpoint, one local lawyer reminds bar and restaurant owners that the way a patron looks or acts during their visit to an establishment matters more than their blood alcohol content (BAC), at least now it does. Take, for example, a woman who had spent around five hours at an establishment, drinking during that time. While it is unclear how many drinks she consumed while there, she left the bar and got into an accident just 200 feet away. Worse yet, she flees the scene.

Now, a significant factor in this case, which is still pending, is whether the patron appeared intoxicated at the time of serving. The former common law claim would have used the theory that the plaintiff was served enough alcohol during that time that the bar should have known their BAC would exceed the limit (.08 or higher). There was even a chart. That law is no longer in effect, in part because alcohol tolerance varies greatly and everyone reacts differently to alcohol. Now that there is no common law claim, they can't simply rely on the BAC to prove the patron was intoxicated due to being over served. In this case, there is video showing there were no noticeable signs of obvious intoxication.

"It doesn't matter what they looked like an hour after the accident," says the lawyer. "It doesn't even matter what they looked like when they left the bar. It's when I handed you the drink." That's the look that matters.

Lessons from the law:
Video is essential, so make sure footage is backed up and stored securely. Note that an establishment is not required to hand over surveillance footage to police until a subpoena is presented.

DELO'S TAKE: Regardless of whether a patron can handle a large amount of alcohol or not, no establishment wants to be responsible for overserving. Teaching staff the signs of obvious intoxication should be a key part of initial and ongoing training. This is another key reason why getting to know your patrons is beneficial.

Here are some key signs of possible intoxication:

- Slurred speech or altered pace of speech, change in speech volume *(becoming loud and uninhibited)*
- Slow, deliberate movement and decreased alertness
- Overly friendly, bothering other patrons, becoming aggressive, or argumentative
- Red, watery eyes or lack of eye focus
- Sweating or flushed face
- Fumbling, falling, stumbling, swaying, or bumping into things or other patrons

Remember, always use tact and diplomacy when a patron needs to be cut off. This can help defuse a potential situation.

DROP DEAD LEGS

SLIP AND FALL LEADS TO A "SHE SAID SHE SAID" SITUATION

A case in Cook County occurred where the plaintiff alleges she tripped when traversing the floor. She alleges there was a piece broken on the transition strip, and she fractured her femur. The waitress said she tripped in a different area where there was no broken piece.

Lessons from the law:
The challenge here is that it's our word versus her word. Had there been video saved showing the fall, we would have a stronger defense. As the video was not saved, there will be a motion filed by the plaintiff for negative inference, which allows a jury to presume the footage would show she fell where she said she did.

DELO'S TAKE: I will always advocate for bars and restaurants to not only have video surveillance but save it for as long as they can.

TROUBLED WATERS

MOTION SENSORS CAN SAVE THE DAY

In a commercial I&B case in Milwaukee County, the tenant above the insured location fell asleep with the bathtub running. Water ran from 6 a.m. until 2:30 p.m. A motion sensor alerted the insured to the water, and cameras show water coming through the ceiling at 6:30 a.m. The bar manager had to pound on the door of the tenant above to get them to wake up and shut off the water.

The tenant was uninsured.

Lessons from the law: Early detection technology can be the difference between a manageable claim and a catastrophic one. The motion sensor helped, but water still ran for over eight hours while staff tracked down the tenant. Without it, the loss could have been far worse.

The uninsured tenant also creates a subrogation problem. The insurer may have a valid negligence claim, but collecting from an uninsured individual is often more trouble than it is worth. Requiring tenant insurance in lease agreements provides a much cleaner path to recovery.

DELO'S TAKE: If it wasn't for the motion detector, this business could have suffered a lot more damage. Take all precautions possible to protect your investment, whether you are there or not.

MEAN STREET

TIMING IS EVERYTHING

This case in Tucson involved two professors, both of whom were deaf, celebrating the end of school at a bar. Because as they were ordering, they communicated by pointing at the menu rather than speaking, the bartender couldn't observe the usual signs of intoxication, like slurred speech or loud behavior. The two men consumed about 12 drinks between them in a relatively short period of time, then drove home separately. One in a car, one on a motorcycle.

There was some suspicion that they were playing cat and mouse on the freeway. Ultimately, they collided, and the motorcyclist was killed. Both had high blood alcohol levels (0.18–0.19). Ultimately, the bar's liability was reduced through comparative fault arguments.

Lessons from the law:
At the time, Arizona law followed common law liability, meaning bars could be held responsible if they served patrons excessive amounts, even without proof of observed intoxication. Today, under statute ARS 4.311, liability requires evidence that bar staff recognized signs of intoxication and served the person anyway (e.g., video or testimony). In this case, no such evidence existed, but the plaintiffs argued based on the number of drinks and BAC levels.

Defense strategies included retrograde BAC calculations and toxicologist testimony. The defense planned to challenge expert opinions through Daubert motions, insisting only direct evidence of visible impairment should matter. Comparative fault played a major role. Blame was apportioned to both drivers: the deceased for choosing to ride drunk, and his friend for also being intoxicated. Typically, juries assign 65 to 85% of the fault to the driver, with the remainder on the bar, but this can shift depending on factors like the drinker's age or level of inexperience.

DELO'S TAKE: The sad truth about this case is that someone's life was lost, and this incident potentially could have been avoided. While the typical audible signs of intoxication may not have given any clues in this case, serving 12 drinks to two patrons in a fairly short time period should have raised a red flag. To slow down rapid consumption, staff could encourage water and food, and potentially slow service, training on additional signs beyond speech (physical cues such as unsteady balance, delayed reactions, glassy eyes, etc.) or refusing service simply based on the high number of drinks between them.

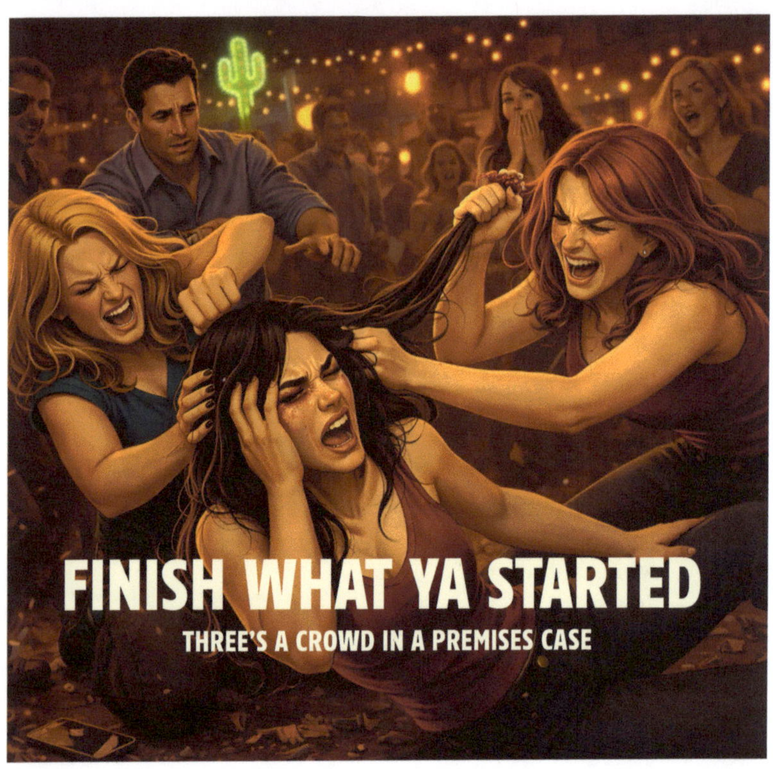

Perhaps some unfinished business from an ex-couple, or too much alcohol, fueled the following situation: a premises liability case at a bar in Tucson that escalated into a bar brawl from an encounter between two exes and one current girlfriend. The trio all happened onto the dance floor at the same time. Then what might have been a friendly exchange between the ex-girlfriend and ex-boyfriend was intercepted by the current girlfriend, who slapped away an attempted fist bump or handshake.

This quickly escalated when one of the ex-girlfriend's friends punched the current girlfriend, who hit the ground, but then got up and went after the ex-girlfriend. Then mayhem ensued: the ex-girlfriend and her friends all ganged up on the current girlfriend, even going so far as cutting her face.

While witness accounts are great in a situation like this, where no establishment staff or security had gotten involved (and could have been held accountable for that), video never lies. Video surveillance was critical in this case as it showed the initial confrontation and slap, the unprovoked punch, and the current

"While witness accounts are great in a situation like this, video never lies."

girlfriend's retaliation: pursuing the ex-girlfriend, which further elevated the situation. Most importantly, it showed the bouncer had no realistic opportunity to intervene. This was crucial in countering any negligence claims regarding failure to act promptly.

Lessons from the law:
In the end, this case was resolved modestly without extended litigation, primarily due to the video, which showed mutual participation versus one-sided victimization and clarified that bar staff couldn't have prevented the fight given how quickly it escalated.

DELO'S TAKE: Without the video, this case could have gone another way, and the establishment could have been held accountable for failing to stop this incident from happening.

Never underestimate the power of video footage because it:

- Weeds out conflicting or unreliable witness testimony.
- Objectively establishes the sequence of events.
- Can protect your business from exaggerated or unfounded claims.
- Can shorten case duration, reduce litigation costs, and lower potential settlement values when it works in the defense's favor.

In volatile environments like bars, having functioning and properly placed video surveillance isn't just helpful, it can be the defining factor in defending against or resolving a lawsuit effectively.

A few years back, there was a case that received a lot of notoriety. Sadly, this involved four people being shot at a local bar in Gilbert. Three of those shots proved deadly. The claims were massive and beyond wrongful death; there was no apparent reason for the shootings. But when you add alcohol to a shooting situation, that presents the risk of punitive damages, whether justified or not.

The case involved a young man who entered the bar alone and had a few drinks. Eventually, he befriended a group of young adults and even sat with them and had a conversation. There was no drama, no yelling, no altercations. No one in the group he had befriended was intoxicated. Then he unexpectedly left, retrieved a gun from his car, returned, and opened fire. Three were killed and one was injured.

The victims were innocent bystanders, and the potential wrongful death claims were estimated to be worth $10-15 million, possibly more, especially considering the involvement of alcohol and the potential for punitive damages.

Surveillance video showed the shooter behaving normally, no aggression, arguments, or alarming signs. He was not visibly intoxicated, and the bar staff had no reason to see

"Surveillance video showed the shooter behaving normally, no aggression, arguments, or alarming signs."

him as a threat. At one point, a bartender did cut him off from further alcohol service (which was not captured on video), but he didn't react violently or draw attention, which is an essential factor. If he had acted violently or slammed his fists on the bar, maybe there could have been a problem. But the video showed he wasn't doing anything like that. He walked in and out of the bar several times, which the plaintiff tried to frame as suspicious, but nothing clearly indicated danger.

The bar's defense leaned heavily on this video evidence, which sadly showed the mayhem of the shooting. Otherwise, it showed nothing egregious or obviously negligent on the bartender's part. This helped reduce liability. Ultimately, the case settled for a fraction of its potential value (maybe around $1 million or less), even though it involved a viable business and a potential excess insurance policy.

Lessons from the law:
There was risk beyond the underlying policy, but it gave us plenty of defenses to get it in a position to settle, thanks to the video, because it doesn't show anything egregious. If it's not egregious, you can describe it with witnesses. But when you see it on video, nothing happened. It's not subject to interpretation.

DELO'S TAKE: Once again, video serves to be crucial in this instance. Unfortunately, it couldn't prevent this situation from happening, but it was able to protect the bar and the bartender, who were just as innocent as the bystanders who became the victims. The video showed the bartender followed protocol by cutting the individual off, even though he wasn't displaying any significant signs of intoxication. In this case, additional cameras around the bar could have been helpful to assess the situation from different angles.

SIGNS OF LIFE

AWARENESS IS EVERYTHING

There was a situation in Cook County where the plaintiff misstepped going out the back door of a premise. She alleged improper lighting. There is a sign on the door that reads, "*Watch Your Step,*" plus the doorman told her to watch her step (which she says distracted her, causing her to miss the sign). Her friend traversed the stairs fine (he was looking down). The video shows that she did not look down. The stairs have some issues, but they are grandfathered in. The video is a double-edged sword; it clearly shows her not looking down, but also indicates a bad fall where she sustained three fractures.

Lessons from the law:
The challenge here is that while it would appear the insured did everything they could, juries tend to want to give money to the injured party despite all of the efforts by the insured. The stairs don't look good, and juries should consider that they are grandfathered in. But again, they have a challenging time ignoring the pictures of the bad stairs and the nasty fall.

DELO'S TAKE: Even though the insured appears to have done everything right (proper signage, a verbal warning from the doorman, grandfathered stairs), optics matter enormously in front of a jury. When jurors see photos of deteriorating stairs and a woman with three fractures, logic takes a back seat to empathy.

The real lesson is that "grandfathered in" should never mean "good enough." Better lighting, updated stair conditions, or additional signage could have eliminated the exposure entirely. The video cuts both ways: it shows she wasn't looking down, but it also captured a serious injury that a jury won't soon forget. The best claim is always the one that never gets filed.

SUCKER PUNCH

BAR FIGHT GONE WRONG

In this case, in Maricopa County, the plaintiff was asked to leave due to his behavior. He was belligerent and pushed another patron, who, in turn, punched the plaintiff in the face. The bouncer put him in a choke hold and then just "dropped" him. The plaintiff sustained a broken jaw from the punch, but then sustained a TBI from being choked and dropped by the bouncer.

Lessons from the law: The initial punch might have been defensible as an unforeseeable third-party act, but the bouncer changed that. A chokehold and drop created a second, more serious injury squarely on the insured, opening the door to negligent hiring and training claims.

Arizona's respondeat superior doctrine holds employers liable for employees acting within their duties, and removing a patron clearly qualifies. The plaintiff's belligerence may factor into comparative fault, but it's unlikely to offset a TBI or the optics of that takedown.

DELO'S TAKE: This goes back to proper training for security personnel. Bar and restaurant owners will benefit by hiring security members who have professional backgrounds in protection, such as law enforcement.

SHOT IN THE DARK

DEADLY ACTIONS

There was an altercation in a bar in Maricopa County. The plaintiff (who was later shot and killed) was asked to leave and was escorted out. However, he remained sitting in his car for 30 minutes, presumably lying in wait for the patron he got into a scuffle with in the bar. When he saw the patron come out of our bar, he approached him to start a fight. The patron went to his car, retrieved a gun, and shot the plaintiff in the head, killing him.

Lessons from the law:
Our challenges here were that security knew he was sitting in his car and not leaving. The police should have been contacted to respond to the situation. The bar's employees testified that they felt it was poorly run and had security issues.

DELO'S TAKE: Absolutely no one wins in a situation like this. Signage regarding *"No weapons"* anywhere on the premises, in the parking lot and before entry into the establishment, should be posted. However, there typically isn't any way to ensure patrons don't have weapons in their vehicles.

REALITY CHECK

WHAT THESE STORIES MEAN FOR YOUR BUSINESS

The stories in this chapter aren't rare incidents. They're reminders of how quickly things can escalate in environments where alcohol, emotions, and large crowds intersect. Every bar and restaurant operator hopes these situations never happen in their establishment.

But hope is not a strategy.

The difference between a manageable claim and a catastrophic lawsuit often comes down to preparation, training, and documentation.

Before moving on, take a moment to ask yourself the following questions:

SECTION 1: QUICK SCENARIO QUIZ

1. An intoxicated patron attempts to harass another guest. A fight breaks out seconds later.

What could most help protect your business in court?

A. Witness testimony from customers
B. Security camera footage
C. The bartender's opinion about what happened
D. Social media posts from patrons

2. A customer claims they were assaulted by security staff.

What is the best protection for the business?

A. Telling the jury the customer was drunk
B. Video evidence showing what actually happened
C. Removing the security guard from the story
D. Hoping the case settles quickly

3. A customer leaves your bar and causes a serious accident shortly afterward.

From a legal standpoint, what matters most?

A. Their blood alcohol level after the accident
B. How many drinks they ordered
C. Whether they showed visible signs of intoxication when served
D. Whether they were a regular customer

4. A fight breaks out between patrons on the dance floor and escalates rapidly.

What evidence is most likely to help your defense?

A. Security incident reports
B. Video showing the sequence of events
C. Statements from bartenders
D. Police reports

Quiz Answers:

1. Correct Answer: B

Video evidence is often the most powerful and objective form of defense in hospitality-related claims.

2. Correct Answer: B

Without video, these cases often become "he said / she said," which can dramatically increase settlement values.

3. Correct Answer: C

Under Arizona law, liability centers on observable signs of intoxication at the time alcohol was served.

4. Correct Answer: B

Video can establish timing, participation, and whether staff realistically had time to intervene.

DELO'S OPERATOR CHECKLIST

ASK YOURSELF HONESTLY:

- ☐ Do we have working security cameras covering entrances, exits, and high risk areas?
- ☐ Do we store footage for at least 30 days? (preferably longer)
- ☐ Are staff trained to recognize signs of obvious intoxication?
- ☐ Do employees know how to cut off a guest diplomatically?
- ☐ Is security trained in de-escalation and proper physical intervention?
- ☐ Do we document incidents and maintain logs when problems occur?
- ☐ Are we proactive about preventing problems and not just reacting to them?

If you answered "no" to even one of these, you may have an exposure you didn't realize existed.

SECTION TWO: EDUCATION

When dealing with a potentially deadly substance (yes, alcohol), it is absolutely crucial to be as knowledgeable as possible about the state's laws. This is for the safety and protection of your business, staff, and patrons. This chapter is our "the more you know" section, designed to give you a quick overview of some of the most common issues related to liquor licensing, coverage, and law.

The information in this chapter was gleaned from some of the most knowledgeable and experienced professionals in the industry: Chuck Onofry, of Schneider & Onofry, P.C., Craig Miller, partner of the Arizona Liquor Industry Consultants (ALIC), and Kevin Grojean, liquor law compliance specialist for the organization. You can read a little about each of them in the resources section at the end of the book.

These are some basic terms you should know, as well as real scenario instances and examples surrounding these terms.

Punitive Damages:

Punitive damages are not designed to compensate victims but to punish defendants for extreme misconduct and discourage similar behavior in the future. In Arizona liquor liability cases, punitive damages are frequently requested but rarely granted. Courts require clear and convincing proof that the defendant's actions went beyond ordinary negligence or simple overservice, such as serving alcohol to someone who is clearly incapacitated (for example, falling off a stool or unable to speak).

Most claims for punitive damages are dismissed before or after trial. Judges typically expect bar staff to respond to visible signs of intoxication rather than measure blood alcohol levels or question patrons extensively. Although many plaintiffs include punitive damages in their claims, claimants mostly overstate their value to a case. In many instances, those claims are dismissed based on insufficient evidence. However, there are instances where there is a legitimate concern, such as where the drink count at a single location is particularly high or where a strip club is involved.

Most insurance policies exclude punitive damages from coverage, making them a concern more in theory than in practice.

Consent Decree:

A consent decree is a legal agreement between a bar (or business) and a government agency, like the Department of Liquor. For example, instead of fighting the case in court, the business agrees to accept specific penalties, such as paying a fine or admitting to specific violations, in order to keep its liquor license.

It's important to understand that signing a consent decree is not just a settlement; it's an official admission of wrongdoing. The agreement becomes part of the public record and can later be used as evidence in lawsuits, even if the business believes it didn't actually do anything wrong.

Chuck explains that the Arizona Department of Liquor sometimes investigates bars and restaurants after incidents such as overservice claims or negligent security cases. He gives the example of a small rural bar that became involved in a fatal altercation after an off-duty assistant manager, who had been drinking, asked a disruptive patron to leave. Even though the bar itself had not overserved anyone and had attempted to de-escalate the situation, the Department of Liquor determined that once the manager acted in an official capacity while intoxicated, she was representing the bar.

The Department gave the bar a choice: sign a consent decree, an agreement admitting to statutory violations under Title 4, along with a fine, or risk losing its liquor license entirely. Although defense counsel might believe the bar had little liability exposure, the consent decree creates an official record of admitted violations, such as overservice or negligent security, which can later be used against the establishment in civil litigation.

Administrative actions can create serious legal and financial consequences, even when the bar's actual responsibility for an incident appears limited.

Exclusionary Language:

Insurance policies that cover liquor liability often contain exclusionary clauses or sublimits that restrict how much coverage is available for certain types of incidents. One common example is the assault and battery sublimit. Instead of a full $1 million policy limit, there may be a sublimit of $50,000 or $100,000 specifically for claims involving fights or assaults. These sublimits can create significant challenges for defense attorneys because legal fees often come out of that same limited amount, leaving little or no funds to cover settlements or judgments.

Some policies also include gun exclusions, which completely remove incidents involving firearms from coverage.

These exclusions are legally enforceable and have been upheld in court. When a firearm is involved, insurers can and often do deny coverage entirely.

In more recent years, insurance carriers have added more exclusions and tighter limits in response to rising claims and payouts. Assault and battery incidents are the most common area where these restrictions appear. In some cases, even umbrella or excess liability policies exclude liquor or assault and battery coverage altogether. Overall, insurers are adhering strictly to these exclusions, and courts generally uphold them since they are reviewed and approved by legal experts before being included in policies.

Dram Shop Lawsuits by the Numbers:

In Arizona, about 95% of Dram Shop cases settle, with only around 5% proceeding to trial. In Maricopa County, less than 1% of the cases are tried to a conclusion.

Cases typically go to trial when damages are extremely high or difficult to evaluate, such as wrongful death, brain injuries, or permanent paralysis, when there are significant disagreements over comparative fault, or when expert testimony conflicts significantly.

Insufficient insurance coverage can also push a case to trial if plaintiffs seek judgments beyond policy limits. Suppose, for example, an insurance company rejects a reasonable settlement demand and a jury later awards damages exceeding the policy limits. In that case, the plaintiff may pursue a separate "bad faith" claim against the insurer, seeking the full amount of the verdict. While insurers can avoid bad faith claims by "opening the limits" and agreeing to pay beyond coverage caps, this rarely happens.

Liability, LLCs, and Owner Responsibility:

How much liability do bar and restaurant owners face in Arizona, especially regarding alcohol service? Owners can usually protect themselves by forming an LLC or corporation and maintaining insurance, which generally limits liability to the business entity rather than the owners personally. However, if corporate formalities are disregarded, such as mixing funds, not holding meetings, or lacking proper records, courts may "pierce the corporate veil," exposing owners' personal assets to lawsuits.

The singular cause of action in Arizona for over-service of alcohol is where the licensee sells alcohol to a customer who is "obviously intoxicated." Thus, the entity which is the license holder is the only correct defendant in these cases. As such, the license should never be held in an individual's name. Most licenses are in the names of an LLC.

Insurance plays a critical role, but if claims exceed coverage limits or the business has no insurance, bankruptcy is often the outcome. While employees, like bartenders, are generally covered under the establishment's insurance, they may face personal criminal charges for extreme overservice or serving minors, which insurance does not cover.

If a bar loses its insurance due to a large claim, it may be forced to shut down and liquidate assets. Owners sometimes attempt to start a new entity with the same liquor license, since licenses retain value. However, they must still disclose past claims honestly to insurers.

Ultimately, maintaining proper corporate structure, adequate insurance, and compliance with liquor laws are the keys to minimizing risk.

Landlord/Premises Liability:

Landlords generally have limited liability when it comes to liquor-related lawsuits, since they aren't the ones serving alcohol and therefore aren't covered under dram shop laws. However, landlords can still face lawsuits in cases involving premises liability, such as slip-and-falls or negligent security. Commercial leases usually protect landlords by requiring the bar to carry significant liability insurance (often between $1-3 million) and include indemnity clauses, meaning the bar must defend and cover the landlord if they are sued.

In rare cases where the bar owns its own building, it's best practice to separate the ownership of the bar and the property into two different LLCs to protect assets and avoid "piercing the corporate veil."

If a bar fails to maintain the level of insurance required in its lease, the landlord (not a plaintiff) can pursue damages against the bar for breach of contract. Landlords usually also have their own insurance policies, but these do not cover liquor liability since they are not serving alcohol.

Best Practices to Mitigate a Claim:

Several key factors can significantly mitigate the outcome of a claim against a bar or restaurant, and the analysis always comes down to how a jury will view the business and its actions. Training is foundational: while not all staff are legally required to be Title 4 certified, jurors expect bartenders to be trained and for owners to enforce their own handbook policies regarding certification. Expired or missing certifications can look negligent and undermine credibility. The demeanor of the owner during deposition is equally critical.

Bar owners frequently do not find out about a claim until months and maybe years later. Therefore, employees rarely remember anything in particular about the night in question, making it difficult to find a friendly witness who can speak favorably for the bar owner. However, if your claim is not settled and goes to trial, you still need to have someone to act as the face of the company. It is crucial not to disengage from your attorney merely because no one at the bar recalls that evening.

Juries often start with skepticism toward bars, and some jurors don't drink or may associate bars with negative personal experiences, so an owner must present himself as a "good corporate citizen."

This means demonstrating clear policies and practices to promote patron safety, responsible alcohol service, and adequate security measures.

Camera footage is another decisive factor that we cannot stress enough. Surveillance can make or break a case, sometimes even leading to outright dismissal if it disproves a plaintiff's claims. While footage can also capture damaging evidence, it is generally better to know the risks early and prepare. Proper documentation, well-run operations, and visible safety measures all help a bar owner credibly argue that they take public safety seriously, which can reduce exposure and foster more favorable jury impressions.

Avoid Bad Practices:

Obviously, focusing on best practices is ideal. But let's take a look at standard bad practices in bars that create liability exposure for the insured (bar owners) and fail to protect themselves from claims. Key issues include serving alcohol during "last call," failing to screen patrons for obvious intoxication, inconsistent ID-check policies, and not adhering to established employee handbooks. These practices can lead to severe consequences, especially in cases where patrons cause accidents after being overserved.

Toxicology and witness testimony can easily demonstrate bar liability, particularly for the last bar a patron visits, so it's imperative to always abide by the law.

Multiple Carriers:

When a bar or restaurant owner purchases general liability (GL) insurance from one carrier and liquor liability (LL) coverage from another, disputes often arise when a claim involves both overservice and inadequate security. For example, if a patron is overserved and later injured in a fight, plaintiffs may sue under liquor liability for overservice and under general liability for failure to provide adequate security.

In these cases, the two carriers often argue over who is responsible, with each pointing to the other to avoid paying. This leaves defense attorneys managing conflicts between insurers while still protecting the bar owner.

The attorney's role is to focus on the total exposure to the client, not to split damages between liquor and general liability.

Ultimately, carriers must work out their share of the settlement, but this slows resolution and complicates mediation.

Plaintiff attorneys benefit from this setup since they can target two separate policy pots, increasing the chance of recovery. Even when only one carrier provides both GL and LL, exclusions in one policy (like assault and battery under LL) may push plaintiffs to pursue claims under the other (GL) to access coverage. Overall, multiple carriers create inefficiency, higher costs, and more uncertainty for insured businesses.

An Insurance Company Hiring an Attorney:

When an insurance company hires an attorney to represent a bar or business, the attorney's client is the insured, the bar, not the insurance company, even though the insurer is paying the bill. The attorney owes the bar all ethical obligations, including confidentiality and zealous representation. At the same time, the insurance company has contractual rights, such as cooperation from the insured and access to information about the case. It's important to note that the insurance company usually has the exclusive right to settle the case.

Unlike doctors, bar owners typically don't get a consent clause to veto settlements.

This arrangement creates a "three-way relationship" between the insured, the insurer, and defense counsel. If coverage issues arise, like whether an exclusion applies, the insurer may file a declaratory action against the insured, and defense counsel cannot represent both sides. The attorney must always remain loyal to the insured, not the insurer. Problems can arise if the bar believes the lawyer is favoring the insurance company over them.

Policy limits create especially tough situations. Defense counsel must give honest evaluations of case value rather than inflating estimates to pressure the insurer into settlement. If the damages could realistically exceed the policy limits, the insurer risks exposure to bad faith claims if it refuses to settle. Large commercial accounts sometimes negotiate "choice of counsel" provisions, allowing insureds to select their lawyer, often from a panel. However, bars rarely have "consent clauses" giving them control over settlements.

Insured's Rights After an Incident:

Another important topic is the insured's rights and best practices after a potential incident occurs. This includes how to handle requests for information, interactions with attorneys, and working with insurance-appointed counsel.

For example, police can request video evidence without a subpoena, and the insured is generally required to provide it.

Insureds have no obligation to speak to attorneys who contact them independently, especially "ambulance-chasing" lawyers, unless they have hired them or the insurance company has formally appointed them.

There are situations where an insured has their own attorney in addition to insurance-appointed counsel. In cases like these, the additional attorney acts as oversight and protection for the client. Proper coordination between insured, insurer, and counsel is critical, particularly regarding policy limits and settlement demands, to prevent exposure to bad-faith claims.

REAL LIFE SCENARIOS

THE ARIZONA LIQUOR INDUSTRY CONSULTANTS (ALIC): AN INVALUABLE RESOURCE

Arizona Liquor Industry Consultants (ALIC) is a leading resource for Arizona's hospitality industry, providing comprehensive guidance and hands-on support to bars, restaurants, and event organizers. Founded more than 30 years ago, ALIC was created to fill a critical gap in the industry, offering practical education, compliance expertise, and licensing assistance to help operators navigate the complexities of Arizona's liquor laws with confidence.

ALIC's services span every stage of the licensing and compliance process. The team brokers quota licenses, such as bar, beer and wine bar, and liquor store licenses, which are limited in number and transferable within each county.

ALIC also acts as a licensing agent, assisting clients with applications, public hearings, and compliance documentation. Beyond licensing, the firm provides compliance inspections, public safety and security plan development, fingerprinting services, and event support for festivals, golf tournaments, and non-profit fundraisers. With extensive experience and strong relationships across state and local agencies, ALIC ensures that each client receives expert, efficient, and personalized guidance.

Education is central to ALIC's mission. The company operates Arizona's largest Title IV liquor law training program, offering classes for bartenders, servers, security personnel, managers, and owners. These in-person sessions are designed to build lasting knowledge, covering essential topics such as responsible service, signs of intoxication, ID verification, and regulatory requirements. By engaging participants directly and allowing for real-time questions and discussion, ALIC's training approach fosters true understanding and helps businesses maintain a culture of safety and compliance.

For many bar and restaurant owners in Arizona, ALIC can become an invaluable long-term partner. Clients rely on the team for continuing education, regulatory updates, and practical advice drawn from decades of combined experience in law enforcement, regulation, and hospitality operations.

With a proven track record of integrity, professionalism, and results, ALIC empowers Arizona's liquor-licensed businesses to operate responsibly, confidently, and successfully.

In this next section, Craig and Kevin walk through common scenarios that bar and restaurant owners often find themselves in.

Common Mistakes Business Owners Make With Liquor Licensing:

If you're opening a restaurant, bar, or any establishment that plans to serve alcohol, securing your liquor license is one of the most important, and often most misunderstood, steps in the process. For many business owners, liquor licensing feels like a minor administrative task compared to building out the space or hiring staff. But in reality, even a slight misstep can delay your grand opening by weeks or even months, costing significant time and money. As Craig and Kevin have seen time and again, the biggest mistakes business owners make with liquor licensing usually fall into a few predictable categories.

Overlooking the Personal Questionnaire:

One of the most common, and easily avoidable, errors occurs before the application is even submitted. Every applicant must complete a personal questionnaire, which includes a detailed section asking whether the individual has ever been cited, detained, or arrested for any reason.

It's a confusing section that often trips people up. Many assume that if they paid a fine or received a citation, it doesn't count as an arrest. But the state's definition is broader than most realize.

People usually think back about a year. But the state requires owners to look back five years, and that's where mistakes happen.

For example, someone might forget about a minor incident, like being cited for public urination at a concert, and fail to disclose it. When the background check turns up the citation, the application gets flagged, and the approval process stalls.

These omissions aren't usually malicious. They're just honest oversights that cause unnecessary delays. Reviewing your personal history thoroughly and being transparent can save weeks of frustration.

Underestimating the Timeline:

Another major mistake is assuming the licensing process moves quickly. According to Craig and Kevin, business owners often come to them two or three months before their planned opening, thinking that's plenty of time. That might have worked a few years ago, but not anymore.

Government processing times have lengthened, and each municipality has its own set of permits, hearings, and inspections that must be completed before a liquor license can be approved. In some cases, a restaurant can be fully built and staffed, yet unable to open because the license is still pending.

The lesson? Start early, much earlier than you think you need to. Build a buffer into your timeline for approvals and unexpected delays. A few extra months of planning can prevent costly downtime later.

Skipping the Research on Property Use:

Many business owners also fail to research their property's zoning and permitted uses before applying. A typical example is adding a patio or expanding outdoor seating.

You might think adding a few tables outside is simple. But if your property isn't zoned for that, you'll need a separate use permit, which often requires a city hearing.

This oversight can bring an otherwise smooth process to a halt. Before signing a lease or finalizing your layout, make sure the property is zoned appropriately for your intended use, both inside and out.

Trying to Navigate the Process Alone:

Another pitfall is the "DIY" approach to liquor licensing. Some owners attempt to handle the process themselves or rely on an attorney unfamiliar with the nuances of state and local liquor laws. In many cases, these owners circle back to ALIC weeks later, frustrated and behind schedule.

They come back to us three or four weeks later. At that point, the only thing they've lost is time, and time is the most valuable thing they have, according to Craig and Kevin.

Hiring experienced professionals who know how to navigate state and city requirements can streamline the process and prevent costly missteps. ALIC's team includes professionals who've worked with the Department of Liquor for more than a decade and maintain daily contact with city offices. Their familiarity with local systems and changes helps clients avoid delays that might otherwise go unnoticed.

Misunderstanding Background Checks and Disclosure Rules:

It's also surprising how often

applicants omit information during background checks, especially when it comes to prior offenses. The state of Arizona doesn't hold a past mistake against you for life. If you had a DUI or made a mistake 10 or 20 years ago, it doesn't automatically disqualify you.

But failing to disclose it can. The state values honesty and transparency far more than perfection. If you made an error in judgment years ago, acknowledge it. Trying to hide it almost always creates bigger problems.

Ignoring the Value of Expert Guidance:

While every business owner's situation is unique, the consensus among industry professionals is clear: trying to navigate the liquor licensing process without expert help is rarely worth the risk.

The team at ALIC prides itself on offering a one-stop resource for every aspect of alcohol licensing and compliance.

Whether it's securing a permanent license, managing a special event permit, handling use permits, or resolving compliance issues, their team has seen and solved it all. There's nothing ALIC won't do when it comes to alcohol. From the simplest question to the most complex licensing scenario, they are there to help. Their experience doesn't just save time, it helps business owners avoid the kind of mistakes that can derail a launch or jeopardize compliance long after opening day. Getting a liquor license isn't just about paperwork, it's about protecting your investment. By learning from the common mistakes others have made, you can move through the process with confidence, clarity, and far fewer surprises.

The Most Overlooked Arizona Liquor Laws That Put Businesses at Risk:

Running a successful bar or restaurant in Arizona requires more than great food, delicious cocktails, and stellar service. Behind the scenes, there's a complex web of liquor laws that govern everything from how you verify IDs to what happens when your team celebrates a busy night. Many of these laws seem minor, but overlooking them can cost thousands in fines, jeopardize your license, and even put your business reputation on the line.

According to Craig and Kevin, many establishments (both new and seasoned) miss the exact critical details. These are the areas where minor oversights can lead to major consequences.

The New Focus on Security Attestations:

A newer area of enforcement that many owners haven't caught onto yet involves security personnel attestations. Every person working security in an establishment with a liquor license must now sign a document confirming that, within the last five years, they have not been convicted of or involved in serious crimes such as assault, sexual offenses, or homicide.

The problem? Many venues don't have these attestations on file, or worse, they don't realize they need them at all.

By law, those signed attestations must be kept onsite at the licensed location, ready for inspection. If the department came in and asked for them, most businesses couldn't produce a single one.

Losing these forms (or never collecting them in the first place) can quickly lead to fines. Hard copies can be easily misplaced, damaged, or accidentally discarded, especially when kept in a busy back office. The best practice is to store digital copies in an organized, easily accessible system that can be produced at any time. This is one of those compliance details that may not seem urgent until an inspector asks for documentation and you don't have it.

Failing to Prove ID Checks:

Everyone knows they're supposed to check IDs. But far fewer owners realize that under Arizona law, it's not enough to simply say you checked an ID. You must be able to prove it.

If a minor sneaks in with a fake ID and is caught, the first question the Department of Liquor will ask your staff is, "Can you show proof you checked the ID?" Without documentation, it's assumed you didn't.

A bartender's word alone doesn't count.

That's why it's crucial to implement systems that record each ID verification, whether through an ID scanner, a written log, or a camera system that captures both the ID and the customer presenting it.

Electronic ID scanners are one of the most efficient tools

available today. They can read the magnetic stripe or barcode on the back of most driver's licenses and store the verification data securely. The technology is also evolving rapidly. Some modern systems even integrate with point-of-sale (POS) devices so servers can check IDs and process transactions seamlessly.

For rural or smaller establishments without scanners, Arizona's Smart ID Verifier app offers a cost-effective option. This state-supported tool lets staff verify IDs by taking a photo, storing the data securely in the cloud, and providing proof of verification without retaining personal customer information.

No matter the system, the key is documentation. If you can't prove the ID was checked, the law assumes it wasn't.

Ignoring Digital IDs:

Arizona has been a national leader in offering mobile driver's licenses through the Motor Vehicle Division's app, but surprisingly few businesses accept them.

Mobile IDs are fully legal and secure, complete with live verification features like subtle movement in the image to prevent screenshots from being used fraudulently. Yet, many bars and restaurants still refuse to accept them, often out of habit or fear of change.

By refusing mobile IDs, establishments not only frustrate guests but also miss out on a more reliable, traceable form of identification. As mobile verification continues to grow, it's only a matter of time before digital acceptance becomes the standard.

Smart operators will adapt early, before the law or public expectation forces them to.

Employees Drinking on the Job:

Perhaps the most common and persistent violation is also one of the oldest: employees consuming alcohol while on duty or after hours.

While it might seem harmless to let your team celebrate a busy night with a drink, Arizona law is strict. No alcohol can be served, poured, or consumed on a licensed premises after 2:00 a.m., and all drinks must be completely cleared by 2:30 a.m.

Each violation (every drink served or held) can result in fines of $750 or more, per person, per incident. And that's just for first-time offenses.

It's easy for what feels like a

small gesture of appreciation to spiral into a costly mistake.

If five employees are celebrating at 2:30 a.m., each drink is its own violation. Even if the cups look empty, but there's still ice in them, that's enough for an inspector to write it up.

During legal serving hours, employees are allowed to have a "shift drink," but only after they're completely off duty (clocked out and no longer performing any work). Even rolling silverware, cleaning tables, or helping the bar while drinking counts as working and therefore violates the law.

Best practices include:

- **Ensuring employees are fully clocked out before consuming any alcohol.**
- **Encouraging them to change shirts or remove name tags to avoid confusion.**
- **Maintaining clear written policies on employee alcohol consumption.**

It's not just about fines, it's about protecting your license and maintaining professional accountability.

Best practices:

Should employees be allowed to drink at their establishment?

One of the most debated topics among bar and restaurant operators is whether employees should be allowed to drink where they work. There's no one-size-fits-all answer, but the most effective policies balance culture, customer relations, and compliance.

On one hand, hospitality is a social business. Guests often want to buy a drink for their favorite bartender or share a toast with a familiar server after a long night. Many owners also want to create a relaxed, team-oriented atmosphere that rewards hard work. But without clear boundaries, that same good-natured culture can quickly lead to overindulgence, poor judgment, or violations of Arizona's liquor laws.

The experts at ALIC offer the following suggestions to maintain that atmosphere for employees while still abiding by the law and staying out of trouble. Their suggested policy:

- **Employees can enjoy up to two discounted drinks *(between 40% 50% off, excluding premium spirits)* after clocking out.**
- **They must be fully off duty, not helping with cleanup or serving, and only while the establishment is still open to the public.**

- **Anything beyond two drinks means heading elsewhere.**

This policy keeps the environment friendly but professional, reduces the risk of post-shift issues, and maintains the respect of both staff and patrons. Allowing limited, structured post-shift drinks can strengthen morale and customer relationships, but only with clear boundaries, written policies, and consistent enforcement. When done right, it supports your culture without putting your liquor license, or your reputation, at risk.

Forgetting Documentation and Record Keeping:

Many of the liquor law violations that lead to penalties could be avoided with better documentation. Incident logs, employee records, and attestation forms tend to "disappear" over time, spilled on, misplaced, or never filled out in the first place.

The best operators know that compliance isn't just about following the law; it's about proving you followed it. Keep a secure, organized system for storing:

- **Security personnel attestations**
- **Incident and employee logs**
- **Proof of ID checks**
- **Training certificates**
- **Correspondence with the Department of Liquor**

These records should be easily accessible, whether stored physically in binders or digitally in secure folders. When inspectors arrive, being able to produce documentation quickly sends a clear message that your establishment takes compliance seriously.

Arizona's liquor laws aren't designed to make life difficult for business owners, they're designed to protect the public and promote responsible operation. But enforcement is strict, and ignorance isn't an excuse.

A single missing form or a misplaced log can turn into thousands of dollars in fines and weeks of lost business. By staying organized, embracing new verification technologies, and educating your staff, you can prevent minor mistakes from becoming major violations. In an industry built on hospitality, compliance may not be glamorous, but it's what keeps your doors open and your business thriving.

SECTION THREE: DELO'S DOS, DON'TS, AND SECRETS OF SUCCESS

I've seen a lot of incidents, justly and unjustly, during my two decades plus of experience in this industry, and I can tell you that it's always, always better to be safe than sorry. Insurance has both come to save the day and served as a headache. But based on my experiences, I want to serve as an advocate and help you understand what is changing, what is stationary, and how to avoid a legal disaster.

These are some of my top "dos and don'ts" to ensure not only your success, but your safety, when it comes to your business, your staff, and your customers.

DO: Get To Know Your Customers

Familiarity matters, from a legal standpoint. Knowing your regulars isn't just good service, it's your frontline defense. A key legal question in many alcohol-related claims is whether someone was "visibly intoxicated" when served. If your team knows your customers well, they're far more equipped to make that judgment accurately. They'll also be able to confidently explain a guest's typical demeanor and flag when something seems off.

But in today's legal climate, you need more than gut instinct. Lawsuits in the hospitality sector are increasingly backed by private funding, giving plaintiffs more leverage to drag out cases and demand larger settlements. Add to that the emotional leanings of juries who often see bars as the "corporate bad guy." Now, all of a sudden, you're on the defensive, even if your team did everything right.

It's About Safety

Customer rapport isn't just a legal shield, it's a tool for proactive safety. By getting to know your regulars, your staff can begin to recognize subtle changes in their behavior. Maybe someone slurs slightly after just one drink. Or perhaps a usually friendly and talkative guest becomes unusually aggressive. These cues can help your staff make smart, potentially life-saving decisions before things escalate.

When you know your customers well, you're more likely to notice if they arrive already intoxicated, an often overlooked liability. With the proper training, your staff can stop the service before the first drink is even poured.

The Profit Perks of a Personal Touch

Getting to know your customers can benefit your business beyond proactive protection. Studies show that increasing customer retention by just 5% can boost profits by 75% to 95%. Regulars not only spend more, they tell their friends, bring new faces, and act as walking advertisements for your establishment. Recognizing them by name, remembering their favorite drink, and creating a welcoming space turn casual patrons into loyal regulars.

Loyalty programs, personalized specials, or even just a warm greeting can create that "third place" experience, where your bar becomes not just a venue but a home away from home for your customers. Training, your staff can stop the service before the first drink is even poured.

DON'T: Underestimate the Power of Security Personnel

Safety starts before a guest even walks through the door, which is why hiring security personnel is essential. Door security helps ensure that only individuals who are of legal age and sober are allowed entry, reducing the risk of incidents from the very beginning. Remember, it is illegal to allow an intoxicated person into an establishment. Trained staff at the entrance can quickly identify signs of intoxication, deny access when necessary, and set the tone for a safe environment inside.

Beyond the front door, security personnel stationed in exterior areas, such as sidewalks or parking lots, play an equally important role. Their presence helps deter disruptive behavior, manage crowd flow, and provide a quick response if a situation arises outside the establishment. By investing in security coverage both inside and outside, bar and restaurant owners can create a safer, more controlled environment that protects patrons, staff, and their business as a whole.

Security personnel should actively monitor for early warning signs of aggressive behavior and have a plan in place for quick response. Hiring trained security staff, such as door personnel or additional team members with prior law enforcement or nightclub experience, can strengthen prevention efforts and help your patrons feel safe and welcome.

Their presence alone can deter issues, and their training allows them to step in early, before a situation becomes dangerous. The power and value of security personnel are definitely not worth underestimating.

Be Proactive and Take a Stance of Safety

Don't sit back and wait for an incident to happen before you realize the steps you need to take to protect your business aren't just for fun. Being proactive in preventing safety incidents is essential. For bar and restaurant owners, protecting your business, employees, and guests requires forward-thinking strategies rather than reactive responses. Particularly in today's climate, where the risk of violence is heightened, it's critical to take steps that minimize potential threats before they escalate.

A strong first step is creating clear boundaries through signage. Posting "no weapons" notices at entry points, on your building itself, and throughout the property, including parking areas, sets expectations immediately. These signs not only discourage unwanted behavior but also reinforce your commitment to safety.

By prioritizing proactive safety measures, you can create a secure and welcoming environment that protects your staff, patrons, and the long-term success of your business.

DO: Train, Overtrain, and Commit to Ongoing Training

(especially liquor protocols and detecting over-consumption)

Once in the door, the responsibility moves from door security to staff and security within the establishment. So it's essential that everyone who is serving alcohol or has been hired to protect your patrons is up to date on proper training and protocols. These should include detecting whether a patron is displaying signs of intoxication, whether they appear to be developing these signs while in your establishment, and what to do when staff or security personnel begin to take note of these signs. Following these protocols can help protect you in a lawsuit.

From there, staff also need to understand how much is too much when it comes to serving. Knowing the warning signs of intoxication, like slurred speech, loud or disruptive behavior, drinking too quickly, or visible signs such as red eyes or a flushed face, can make all the difference. And remember, it's illegal to serve someone who is already intoxicated, regardless of whether they're driving or not.

Of course, no bar or restaurant owner enjoys the idea of cutting someone off, but these safety steps aren't optional, they're essential. Allowing an intoxicated person to leave and possibly get behind the wheel puts lives at risk, including your own liability as the business owner.

That's why ongoing education is so important. Employees need to know how liquor laws work, how to recognize intoxication, and exactly what actions to take when they see the warning signs. This starts with thorough training on how to spot intoxication before someone even enters your establishment and continues with monitoring throughout their visit.

Make it a priority to keep yourself and your staff current on liquor laws and industry requirements. Regulations and hospitality standards are constantly evolving, and regular training ensures your business stays compliant, protected, and above all, safe.

DON'T: Misplace Documentation

It's not enough to simply have the proper documentation, certifications, and licensing. You need to be prepared to produce that paperwork on a moment's notice when the time comes. You not only need proper coverage, you need to be able to prove it. This paperwork is a line of defense that helps you protect your business from a lawsuit.

Document everything, keep it organized, and within arm's reach (but in a safe place). Know where it is at all times and be able to easily access it.

If you get wind of an incident happening, even if you're unsure whether that person was at your establishment within the time period, collect your camera footage and save it. Whether or not you are potentially liable, it's essential to have it on hand, particularly in the case of a car accident, injury, or death near your establishment. Timestamped footage from your security cameras can truly be a lifesaver.

DO: Turn on the Cameras *(inside and out)*

If you learned anything from the stories in section one, please let it be the importance of video footage in and around your establishment. This is a solid safety and security strategy for everyone involved and for your business.

The use of surveillance cameras in and around your property is vital. Timestamped video surveillance can serve as crucial evidence in the case of an incident, whether that is a fall in the kitchen or a service customer altercation. Producing video in a court of law that showcases the details of an incident can limit your liability. In a best-case scenario, it can absolve your establishment of any wrongdoing in the case of an incident.

DON'T: Ghost Your Insurance Agent

Don't think of your insurance coverage as a footnote or put it off until the last minute. It's not something to simply cross off your list. It could be one of the most important things you do for your business. God forbid there is a loss, you want to make sure you're covered.

It's essential to sit down with your insurance provider to review your coverage, ask questions, and understand your potential exposures. Insurance can be a lifesaver in the event of major losses, but it's just as crucial to know what isn't covered. Insurance isn't a maintenance plan for things like air conditioning or refrigeration, it's designed for sudden, accidental property damage, liability incidents, and liquor liability issues. It's essential to work with an insurance agent who specializes in the bar and restaurant industry (like me!).

Not going to a broker who specializes in bar and restaurant insurance is like going to a dentist about your back pain. Sure, he's a doctor. But he's trained to examine your teeth, not your back. Seeing a specialist in the right specialty makes a world of difference in the outcome.

We live, eat, and breathe bar and restaurant insurance, and all our employees have been here for a decade or more. We go through training and classes, too, ensuring we can guide you to the best protection for your needs. Agents like us that specialize in hospitality businesses are going to be best equipped to handle your unique situations because they know the ins and outs of the industry. They will have the knowledge to support your needs and also ensure that you have the coverage that is critical for protecting your business, your staff, and your clientele.

But shameless plug aside, you should also keep the doors of communication open with your agent. If you make a significant change in your business or purchase large pieces of equipment, you need to let them know. It's also a good idea to sit down with your agent at least once a year to review your current policies and make adjustments to suit where your business currently is and where it is going. But there is never a wrong time to revisit your insurance policies to ensure they are airtight.

Maintaining best practices starts with a good line of defense, and your policies are key. If you're new to the business, have an agent skilled in the bar and restaurant industry review your lease and other important documents. A trusted agent can become an integral part of your company's success. So don't be afraid to reach out to them and to seek their advice. There is endless value in forming a solid relationship with your agent. That very concept is what I have built my business on, and I stand by it today.

Partnering with the right people is essential to achieving your goals and sustaining growth. Building a relationship with a specialized broker built on trust, open communication, and mutual respect can provide lasting support and guidance, helping your business move forward with confidence.

DO: Take Caution with Discounts and Promotions

Of course, you're in business to make money, among other things. No one can fault you for that. But when you operate a company that sells alcohol, you have to be particularly careful in the way that you present your discounts and promote specials when it comes to beer, wine, and spirits.

Happy hours, power hours, reverse happy hours, two-for-ones, etc., these are all great ways to bring in customers and boost sales. But these specials can put your establishment at risk.

Avoid reverse happy hour, last call specials, or anything that promotes end-of-night or pre-closing discounts. These promotions could be seen as encouraging your customers to order more alcohol at a discounted price before they have to leave at closing time in just 30 minutes or so. Not a good look in a court of law.

ADDITIONAL "DOS": Follow These Additional Protective Protocols

You may not be able to control every experience that happens within your establishment, but these protocols can further reduce the problems associated with the consumption of alcohol while protecting your staff, patrons, and business:

- **Display staff code of conduct**
- **Display patron code of conduct**
- **Create procedures for last call**
- **Maintain ongoing alcohol training for staff and safety training for security officers**
- **Partner with rideshare companies to ensure safe rides home**
- **Post a no firearms sign**
- **Monitor patterns of consumption**
- **Enact strict underage ID check**
- **Choose interior design that mitigates violence**

SECTION FOUR: RESOURCES

This section is all about quick and useful resources. Tips, checklists, and sample forms that you can reference at any time are all pulled together here in one spot. Think of it as your shortcut guide, whether you're double-checking requirements, prepping for an inspection, or just need a refresher. The goal of this section is to inform you and save you time while helping you feel more confident navigating the liquor licensing process.

12 TIPS FOR BARS AND RESTAURANTS THAT SERVE ALCOHOL IN ARIZONA

1. Liquor can be served between 6 a.m. and 2 a.m.; last call is no later than 1:45 a.m.
2. No alcohol can be consumed on premises after 2:30 a.m.; drinks must be taken between 2-2:10 a.m.
3. In order to be served alcohol, a customer must produce a valid ID if asked by a staff member of an establishment.
4. An obviously intoxicated individual can legally stay in a bar for 30 minutes from the time the state of intoxication is known. This allows time to arrange for proper transportation from the premises.
5. If a customer is obviously intoxicated, work with them to find proper and safe transportation.
6. It is illegal to provide more than 50 ounces of beer, one liter of wine, or four ounces of distilled spirits to an individual at one time.
7. Primary rule of service: When in doubt, don't serve.
8. If a staff member suspects a guest is potentially intoxicated, it is imperative that they notify a manager and coworkers immediately and follow procedures to determine whether or not this is the case.
9. All employees must attend and comply with the State of Arizona Title 4 Training Class.
10. It is mandatory for servers to keep track of how many beverages a patron has consumed. Bartenders working in teams should refer to the guest's tab or a drink tally and utilize a BAC chart to avoid overserving.
11. Servers and bartenders must identify all guests who will be receiving an alcoholic beverage before a round is served.
12. Remember the common signs of intoxication: Loud and/or slurred speech, ordering drinks rapidly, stumbling, spilling drinks, aggressive behavior, and lack of coordination. Many other signs are covered in Title 4 Training.

LIQUOR INSPECTION CHECKLIST
(Developed in Partnership with ALIC)

AT THE BAR

- ☐ Is your license at the bar and clearly visible?
- ☐ Do you have a fetal alcohol warning sign placed within 20 feet of each register?
- ☐ Are only authorized IDs used when verifying age?
- ☐ Is liquor stored only in authorized places?
- ☐ Is there any unauthorized alcohol on premises?
- ☐ Are you refilling or reusing liquor bottles?
- ☐ Are the draft beer spigots properly labeled?
- ☐ Are you offering alcohol on credit?

EMPLOYEE INFORMATION

- ☐ Is your employee log up to date? Does everyone serving alcohol have their Basic Title 4 Certification?

LICENSE

- ☐ Is your license current?
- ☐ Are the ownership, agent manager, and business name and address listed correctly?
- ☐ Are your food sales above 40% of total sales?

PROVIDED BY WHOLESALERS

- ☐ Did your bar mats, fruit trays, glassware, etc. come from an authorized wholesaler or producer?
- ☐ Has a wholesaler or producer provided you with anything over $700?

OPTIONAL, BUT RECOMMENDED

- ☐ Do you have a NO FIREARMS ALLOWED sign posted near the entrance?
- ☐ Does your bar manager or anyone ordering alcohol for your establishment have a Manager Title 4 Certification?
- ☐ Does your social media, ads, specials creator have a Manager Title 4 Certification?

AD AND SPECIALS CHECKLIST

ARE YOU LEADING WITH FOOD?

It is imperative that you focus your specials on food first, then alcohol.

For Example:

YES: Burgers and Beers Monday

YES: Tacos and Tequila Tuesday

NO: Bottle and Bruschetta Night

ARE YOU OFFERING FREE ALCOHOL?

It is illegal in the state of Arizona to offer free alcohol. You can still offer deals and discounts, but proper phrasing is crucial in ads and promotions.

Such As:

YES: 1 Cent Refills

YES: Two for One

NO: Buy One, Get One Free

NO: Unlimited Mimosas

BUSINESS COMPLIANCE INSPECTION FORM

Below is a sample form from the ALIC and Bar and Restaurant Insurance:

Business Name: ______________ Location: ____________________

Inspector Name: _____________________ Date:______________

Inspection Checklist:
Please indicate compliance status for each item and provide comments where necessary.

Item No. Inspection Criteria ☐ Yes ☐ No ☐ NA

Comments

1. Is the liquor license prominently displayed in accordance with regulatory requirements?
2. Is the firearms prohibition signage posted in a location that is clearly visible to patrons?
3. Do purchase invoices confirm procurement from authorized and approved vendors?
4. Is there an up-to-date employee log available? If not, has assistance been provided to achieve compliance?
5. If security personnel are present onsite, is their deployment appropriate and aligned with safety protocols?
6. Is there an incident log, and has it been maintained? If new, has guidance been provided on its establishment and utilization? If existing, has it been reviewed for standard practices?
7. Are procedures in place for handling and storing confiscated fake identification documents?

THANK YOU

THANK YOU FOR READING THIS BOOK, AND THANK YOU FOR THE WORK YOU DO.

To all my friends and coworkers that contributed, you are valued and appreciated.

Hospitality is all about giving, and we know how much you give when you operate a bar or restaurant, or when you work at one. It can be grueling and relentless work. It can be thankless at times.

But I hope the pages in this book and the work I do through Healing Hospitality serve as a small thank you for all you do, and for everything that you give to the hospitality industry in Arizona.

Whether you already own a bar or restaurant or are looking to open one, the contribution you will be providing to the community through good food, great drinks, and social connection is invaluable. The spaces you are creating for celebrations and connections are so crucial for our society. I appreciate what you do and know your job is not easy.

I want this resource to help you, to put your mind at ease, and to protect you from the worry and legal ramifications that are rife in this business. We know you are not just another bar, another restaurant. We are here to share experiences, successes, passion, and life. And we do that through hospitality. It's beyond business. It's personal. And I'm always here to help.

Connect with me through BarAndRestaurantInsurance.com
I look forward to hearing from you.

ABOUT THE AUTHOR

David "DELO" DeLorenzo is the founder of Bar & Restaurant Insurance and owner of Ambassador Group Insurance, specializing in insurance solutions for bars, restaurants, and hospitality businesses. With more than two decades in the industry and hundreds of hospitality clients across Arizona, DELO has built a reputation as a trusted advisor who understands the unique risks restaurant and bar owners face.

If you own or operate a bar or restaurant and want to ensure your business is properly protected, reach out to DELO and his team.

David "DELO" DeLorenzo
Bar & Restaurant Insurance
Ambassador Group Insurance

CONNECT WITH DELO

BarAndRestaurantInsurance.com
ddelorenzo@ambassadorins.com
480.776.6981

ON THE DELO

Arizona Restaurant & Hospitality Stories

Step inside **ON THE DELO Podcast**, where DELO sits down with chefs, restaurateurs, brewers, and the sharpest minds in the industry for raw, unfiltered conversations you won't hear anywhere else. This isn't just another business show. It's real stories from the front lines of hospitality: the wins, the struggles, the mindset shifts, the community, and what it truly takes to build something that lasts.

From insurance and liability to health, leadership, culture, and the day-to-day realities of running a bar or restaurant, DELO keeps it honest and actionable.

If you loved **RISKY BUSINESS**, this is where the conversation continues.

Stay protected. Stay inspired. Stay connected.

Subscribe now! Join the growing community of bar and restaurant owners who refuse to learn the hard way.

www.ingramcontent.com/pod-product-compliance
Lightning Source LLC
LaVergne TN
LVHW052257100826
845147LV00001B/68